DANCE WITH GOD

By
W. NORMAN COOPER

Published by
DeVorss & Company
P O Box 550
Marina del Rey, CA 90291, U.S.A.

ISBN: 0-87516-468-4
Library of Congress Catalog Card Number: 81-69932

Cloth edition ISBN: 0-87516-491-9

Printed in the United States of America

A MESSAGE TO THE READER

7115772

The thoughts which make up this book were first shared with those who attended meetings sponsored by Truth Center, a Universal Fellowship. Because they were so helpful and inspiring to us and to others who heard them, the Fellowship wished to have them preserved in book form and presented to a wider audience.

Our Teacher uses words sometimes in a different manner. He also uses capitalization in a unique way. Some of the statements may call upon you to give up preconceived ideas as to the meaning and use of words. If this is done, new and helpful truths will unfold.

Words which are synonymous for the word God are capitalized. Words which refer to what God does are not capitalized. When referring to the God-created Self, the word Self is capitalized. The word self, when referring to mortal man is not capitalized. In some cases the author has coined words in an attempt to convey his meaning.

A space is left between each thought so that you may make notes regarding the unfoldments which may come to you.

We are publishing this book by our God-inspired Teacher with the hope and prayer that the truths contained in it may bless you as they have blessed and inspired us.

Truth Center, a Universal Fellowship

6940 Oporto Drive
Los Angeles, CA 90068, U.S.A.

INTRODUCTION

One of the sayings I shared in one of my seminars was "Dance with God; but be sure to let Him lead." Of course I was talking symbolically. I was talking of the unity you should have as you go through life—as you dance through life—with God guiding your every step.

It is helpful to remember that dance has played a part in religious worship from the beginning of time. In fact, through most of human history, dance and religion have been inseparable.

Dance played a part in the lives of the people of the Old Testament. The people danced—especially, if not exclusively, during their good times. For instance, when the Ark was brought into Jerusalem, King David—wearing the garments of the priests— "danced before the Lord with all his might" (II Samuel 6:14).

In the New Testament we are told that Jesus rebuked his quarreling contemporaries whom he said were like children who refused to dance. (See Luke 7:31,32.)

The early Christians used not only song but also dance to express their innermost spiritual feelings. Unfortunately, in more modern times, religious people—particularly Protestants—have often frowned on dancing, and so today, dancing is thought of mostly as entertainment or merely a social custom.

Dancing was, and perhaps should be, a part of our religious experience. Dancing can be an outward symbol of our being bound to God—of our being moved by and with God. Through dancing the enthusiasm of our being one with God may be expressed. Even more than dancing as a human act is the symbolic importance which it can be to us. We should learn to dance for and with God. We should feel His presence with us in the movement of the dance.

Dancing could be—and perhaps should be—an outward symbol of the glorious truth that it is with Him that "we live, and move, and have our being" (Acts 17:28).

DANCE WITH GOD

Dance with God, but be sure that you let Him lead.

God is that which has no definition and needs none.

God is the ultimate being, reality and energy of the universe.

To the spiritually enlightened, God seeking him and his seeking God are the same.

God cannot be held in the world of objects—not even in the highest of objects.

God must be so close to us that there is not even a single thought separating us.

We are to put up our swords. We are to refuse to place any dependence upon material means of defending ourselves. This is so because God is ever our weapon of defense. He is the source of our protection.

Spirit cannot—and need not—conquer matter. God is. He is both the source of what we call matter and what we call spirit. He is all.

God is. Nothing can contain Him. He is not in anything but He contains all.

You respond to evil because you believe it to be outside of yourself. When you see that evil is within —as goodness is also within—you will respond to it by returning good for evil.

Life's great struggles provide opportunities in which the self-centered, willful self may die, for only as this death takes place can you behold the eternal life of your divine Self.

One word of a spiritual teaching lived is worth a million words of a teaching taught.

There has never been and will never be a good war. There has never been and will never be a bad peace.

Death is but the giving of ourselves back to God from whence we came.

To die before death is to experience everlasting life here and now.

Faith is the gift of God. Reason is the gift of ungodliness.

We should fight with but one enemy—the ignorance within ourselves which makes us believe we have an enemy. An enemy is someone whom we believe is not expressing the fullness of God's goodness.

Hatred is never overcome by hatred; malice by malice; or war by war. Hatred, malice and war are overcome by love—love which finds its source and reality in Him who is love. The eternal law is that love is the master of hatred, malice and war.

To encourage others to be righteous and not to live righteously yourself is to shut yourself off from the God who is all-righteousness.

To seek a divine teacher outside of yourself is to remain in ignorance.

The voice of Silence speaks of that which must forever remain inaudible. What is said cannot be heard by you, but as you.

God is the one whom everyone knows by name but who actually has no name.

The highest activity you can engage in is silent activity, non-reasoning activity, non-doing activity, actionless activity.

Those who seek the kingdom of God first, experience its peace. Those who seek it second have but a woeful experience.

To enter the kingdom of God means that you let God's will be done in you and as you.

You have only as much faith as you live.

"Faith without works is dead" (James 2:20). Faith not lived is death to our spiritual development.

You have all the power you truly need when you center your whole being in the God-power within.

God is All-in-all. This does not mean that God is where you are; but you are where God is.

Spirit—not matter—is the essence of all genuine life.

You believe that some day you will behold God. You cannot behold God; you must humbly let God behold you.

If you but let Him, God will lead you step by step into a greater awareness of your inwardness.

Only God knows what God is. You can know God only as you are at-one with Him—as you let Him reveal Himself to you.

You cannot build a temple to God. He has already built you as His temple.

True prayer is not a petition to God for His blessings and love; it is the surrender of yourself to Him and to His will for you.

Hell is mortal thought run rampant.

Genuine peace is more than the cessation of war. Genuine peace is the truth of God expressing Itself as peacefulness.

Kinship with nature is most desirable. But such kinship can be found only through a silent and righteous view of beauty and eternity.

The human mind likes everything to be made convenient, easy and comfortable. The divine Mind demands redemption for mere human convenience, ease and comfort. It demands that you find your all in your God.

Every religion has some element of truth in it. Every religion also has some elements of error in it. The only genuine religion is the religion beyond religion—beyond religious teachings and beliefs. Genuine religion can be viewed only in lives lived in accordance with God's will.

Go to the mount of spiritual inspiration and reside there. If you do, you will experience the Love which is beyond loving, the Truth which is beyond truthfulness and the Life which is beyond living.

Selfless labor is a sacrifice to divine love.

Genuine work is selfless love made visible.

Selfless work is the highest form of prayer.

The good news of Easter is not so much that you will be immortal, but that in your present life you can be, and are, at-one with eternal Life—at-one with the God of all life.

Eternal life is not a teaching about the continuity of life; rather, it should be the truth lived at this very moment as your life.

Resurrection is God continuously resurrecting in you the eternality of divine Life.

Easter does not prove that life is immortal. Immortality cannot be proved. It must be lived. It must be gained through God-given faith. You can have the boundless faith that you can live the immortal life here and now.

Eternity is the now-living of the continuity of the life which is God.

The message of Easter is not so much that you shall live gloriously and anew after death, but that you can live gloriously and anew the life which is God in your present life.

Nothing spiritual has a future. It only has a now.

All life is continually unfolding into divine Life.

God is the circle everywhere—the circle which has no circumference.

Even though you ignore Divinity you cannot separate yourself from It.

Peace will not come with the ending of war. Peace comes when it is realized that everyone and every nation has been created unto God, Himself. Until this realization comes, the hearts of men will find no lasting peace.

War is but an extension of the erroneous premise that right can be established by might.

Inspired prayer is more than meditation. It is communion. Through inspired prayer you commune with Him who is All-in-all to you.

Genuine religion is more than a teaching about love. It is that which inspires the living of Love. Without this living of Love, religion becomes but a faint echo of the love which the God of love has for you.

All religions are gifts of God. No religion should be declared to be false. No religion should be condemned. The end of all religion is to glorify God. Respect this unseen end and not the religion's visible mistakes. Respecting another's religion is respecting yourself.

There can be no distinction between good and bad religions; between true and false teachings; between right and wrong doctrines. To the adherent of any religion, his religion is true and good to him. There must be respect for everyone's religion as surely as there should be respect for everyone's spiritual identity.

Some religious teachers believe that the beginning of religion is the love of one's fellowman. Actually, the beginning of all inspired religion is its call to its adherents to find and be one with the Source of one's identity. Genuine love will then flow from this finding and this being of one's oneness.

To declare yourself to be the idea of Divinity is to utter a half-truth. You are to become aware that you are more than an idea. You are at-one with divine Truth. You are to be at-one with the Truth behind the idea. You, yourself, are to be the Truth-in-action.

The act of giving an offering at a religious service is—or at least should be—the outward symbol of the inward act of making your offering to Divinity. To offer to Divinity is to free you from separation from the Source of your being. To offer to Divinity is to declare that you are at-one with the Giver of all substance.

Unfortunately truth is usually thought of as the truth of things as they are perceived by the human mind. Inspired religion calls upon its followers to express Truth—to be the Truth which is independent of the evidences of the human mind or the physical senses. It is this Truth—actively perceived—which enables you to have freedom to be free. "Ye shall know the truth, and the truth shall make you free" (John 8:32).

To do Divinity's will for you is to be at peace. To violate Divinity's will for you is to be deprived of peace.

The end of your being is spiritual oneness with divine Love. In Love you become God-in-action.

There is no great advantage in living unless you live to know the Source of life—and that you know you are created to live for this divine Source.

All acts should be performed as worship to God and must be free from the desire to know the results of the acts.

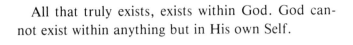

All that truly exists, exists within God. God cannot exist within anything but in His own Self.

God is that which knows all—past, present and future—but can never be known. God can only be lived.

God is activity. He is doing, being, creating, existing. You would gain a clearer view of God if you considered the word God a verb rather than a noun.

You may have a belief in the untrue, but you can only know Truth.

Truth is unaltered by your belief or disbelief in it.

The greatest gift you will ever be able to give to your God is to so uplift yourself that you can rightly care for His children.

Only when the thinking mind is completely silent will you hear Divinity talk to you.

You have a calling in life. Your calling is to patiently wait for God's will to be unfolded for you and once it is unfolded, to act upon it.

Truth can only be expressed. It cannot be possessed. If you endeavor to possess it you will lose its grandeur, beauty and usefulness. If you endeavor to possess truth it will become less than truth to you.

Love will overcome war only if the love is God-created and complete.

You have no personal gifts of value to give to others. All you have to give is what you have received from Divinity and belongs to Divinity.

You find your divine Self—not through memory —but by being spiritually ready so that God can reveal Himself through you.

Genuine devotion is complete resignation to your God in order that He may work through you and as you.

You have been created to return to your Creator.

Avoidance of tribulation is part of the worldly man's life. Submission to tribulation is part of the holy man's life.

If you are to truly share God's word you cannot decide with whom you are going to share it. It is God who makes such a decision. It is your duty to discover His decision and act upon it.

You are not a fallen sinner. You are—and have the potential to be—the risen saint.

The highest meditation is beyond all effort or reason.

The highest life is the life lived as mystical contemplation of God.

To be your divine Self you must be free from ego or desire. You must let God be you-in-action.

All genuine government finds its seat of authority in God. All other government finds its seat of authority in persons and personality and must of necessity eventually lead to tyranny.

You will find that laughter will be a great help in your spiritual development. We are told that Abraham doubled up in laughter when he learned that his aging wife was pregnant. Several of the Psalms picture God as laughing. (See Psalms 2:4; 37:13; 59:8.) If you would lighten your journey Spiritward, learn to laugh.

It has been suggested that part of a verse in Philippians might be rendered: "Death is a prize to be won" (Philippians 1:21). Then death is never really an enemy. It is the fear of death that is an enemy. Would that we were taught that death was a prize to be won as the result of a life well lived.

It is a mistake to look for truth outside of yourself. Also it is really a mistake to look for truth inside of yourself. You must look for and find truth as your divine Self.

You can't really look for truth. Truth can only be lived.

To do God's will requires more than a desire to do it. It requires complete obedience to God's will for you. To be obedient you must be completely absorbed into the One. Then you are the Self being obedient to the Source of obedience.

You cannot really find God; God is ever finding you. You are lived by God. You cannot make yourself spiritual; God is ever existing in you as spirit.

Nothing can be added to spiritual existence. Nothing can be taken from spiritual existence.

You are not a part of God. You are not like a piece of a whole banana. Correctly seen, you are the whole of God.

Learn to say "yes" to God.

The One unites the two. The One unites non-being with being, life with death, activity with non-activity.

The One unites, but you are not to be attached to this unity. You are to be at-one with the One.

All knowledge is delusion. You cannot really have a knowledge of or about your divine Self. You can only live your divine Self.

"I want" is never included in the inspired language of the One. "I AM" is the reality lived by the individual inspired by the One.

When you find your oneness with the One, all doubts will disappear. When this occurs you will no longer avoid doing what is disagreeable to you nor will you seek to do only what is agreeable to you.

Avoid making moral judgments regarding others. God didn't make Christ Jesus a judge and God hasn't made you a judge either.

God's power is unlimited. It cannot be quenched. Do not try to limit His power.

What is prayer? It is the pouring out of the heart to God.

The saint is the one who has a heart big enough and pure enough to respond to God's call to Him to be in His service.

If you do not comprehend the glory of life you will not comprehend the glory of death.

The ultimate essence is Awareness-in-itself.

Your spiritual Awareness is your ruler of your heaven and earth.

You are united to your God by love—and only by love.

For spiritual development you must pass from learning and reasoning into exploration and adventure—and finally into spiritual Awareness. In this Awareness you will be completely free from or the need of learning, reason, exploration or adventure.

Talk to God with the greatest simplicity possible. Avoid intellectual or theological terms. Avoid established prayer. God hears only that which comes from the simplicity of the heart.

Pray to God as if you were aware of the truth that you already belonged to Him.

Prayers are best which are free from the multiplicity of words. A life lived in obedience to God's will for you will bring you closer to Him than even the most beautifully worded prayer.

No nation is God's country. God's country is within you—or more accurately—is you. It is the spiritual realm where God is the governor and you are the governed.

Do not talk about God a lot; but live God a lot.

Go beyond the literal text of Scripture and there discover the spirit and reality of the Word.

If you are to advance Spiritward you must cease desiring worldly rewards. All you need—all you can have—all that you will eventually express—is to be found in your oneness with the one Spirit. Seek for nothing else—have no desires for anything else but your oneness.

Never tell another how busy you are. Never tell yourself how busy you are. You are in God's service and He will not permit you to be overworked or underworked. If you talk to another or to yourself about your busyness you will be burdened by your activities. And you cannot accept God's further work if you are burdened.

You are to be confident that since God has called you into His service He will sustain you in it. It is God's work—not yours. When you say that you have too much to do, you blaspheme. You are one with God; does He have too much to do? Since you are doing God's work there must be no feeling—and certainly no talking—about how busy or overworked you are. "Be still, and know that I am God" (Psalms 46:10). Be still and know that you are to express the I AM, God in your daily work.

Your destiny is to become lost in your awareness of the One.

Reality is what non-thinking awareness recognizes as God.

Being a passerby is synonymous with non-attachment, but not with detachment. You are attached to the One and to all the One creates.

As you grow spiritually you will be changed. Something in you will die in you. Other things will be born—or perhaps be reborn—in you.

You should pray to God because you already belong to God.

Let simplicity in all things be your way of life.

Walk through life with great simplicity.

Forgiveness is the path to rebirth.

It is not God who needs you. It is you who need God. God exists with or without you. But He actually exists with you and in you. He exists and shows His existence to you by permitting you to share His love with others.

You are fulfilling your divine destiny when you express the activity of stillness and the stillness of activity.

You will seek for truth—but what you will find will be God.

All acts of human love should be outward symbols of acts of love done for the Source of divine love.

The One alone is and anything which you attempt to add to this One cometh of evil.

As a person you do not have—nor can you orig-
inate—healing power. Healing power is of God.
The power is God's. Through your prayers this
power appears to be transmitted to others. This
transmitting of God's power is what is called spiritual healing.

Give yourself to the One. The One is always
ready to receive you and to receive you just as you
are.

When you selflessly pray for others you make the prayer "as in heaven so on earth" a living reality.

Love is not so much to be spoken of as it is to be lived.

You are destined to enter the spiritual realm where non-being bespeaks of being and being bespeaks of non-being; where emptiness bespeaks of allness and allness bespeaks of emptiness; where the two are made one in you. When the two are thus made one in you, you will have found and will be living perfection.

You really have no personal gifts to give to others. Every good gift and every perfect gift which you will ever receive or give comes from the One.

The One is all. There can be no "outsidedness" to the One. You cannot avoid being included in the One. You are one with the One. It is the one Father in you which fathers the mighty works you are hourly and daily being called upon to perform.

You are to see good. You are to see evil. You are not to be attracted to or repulsed by either. When you are free from such attraction and repulsion, you are your divine Self.

You cannot really believe in the truth. There is not really a believing mind to know truth. There is only the One knowing the allness of Truth.

You must go into all the world and preach—not because others need what you possess—but because you must include everyone in your spiritual universe.

Mysticism is being united with—and being reunited with—your divine Self as your individual and impersonal identity.

To live the Self means to be released from all relationships or dependence upon anyone or anything other than God, Himself.

Even the slightest willful thought shuts you out from being your divine Self.

God already includes you in His allness. Then, for you to be at-one with Him does not mean that God must add something—you—to Himself.

Allness is not addition. Allness is spiritual inclusion. You are already included in His power-established allness.

Only he is completely free who is no longer caring about externals such as human necessities, possessions or processes.

Faith is not something which you can gain once and for all. Rather it is the sterling quality that you gain—only to lose in order that you may gain new faith—which in turn must be lost in order that still newer faith can be gained.

Be absorbed into God; then you will find that God doesn't actually absorb you. Rather He marries you and you marry Him.

You can give nothing to God. The Psalmist said that God does not require sacrifice and offerings. (See Psalms 40:6.) The only gift God can accept from you is the gift He has already given to you— yourself.

The definition of time: Measurement of re-occurrence.

To spend time gathering external things is to separate yourself from your Self.

By clinging to external things or persons, you are a part in bringing about that which is wicked and ignorant.

You are not destined to fall in love, but you are destined to be in Love.

You should not be a spectator looking out upon God's works. You should be a participant in His works.

You behold the greatness and beauty of the divine Self in God's own view of the allness and oneness of your being.

Truth is given to all. Truth is universal. Truth is not the monopoly of any religion, race or teacher. Truth is. It exists in all.

God can create only out of Himself. His creation is unfolding actively. He creates Himself in you. You are the ever old, ever new creation of God. You exist as His existence. You love as He loves. You are as His "isness."

You are destined to discover the essential in the non-essential and the non-essential in the essential.

Let yourself be a sacrifice for the sake of the Self.

You are destined to respond to your deepest spiritual instinct which tells you that there is reality beyond what the human mind classifies as good and evil, right and wrong, moral and immoral.

You have been called to speak God's word in season and out of season. But it is not you who speaks. It is the spirit of God speaking through you. (See Matthew 10:20.) You are to let God speak to you, through you and as you.

You may hear the voice of God in the still, small voice; you may also hear His voice in God's thunder.

Guru and teacher are synonymous terms—both meaning teacher. But there is one great and important difference in the use of the words. To the Westerner, one may have many teachers helping one Godward. To the Easterner, one selects and has but one guru to help him in his search for God.

At your present state of spiritual development you may not be able to give up human activity completely. But you can start, for only when action ceases will you be your Self. Then you will be the non-action of the active One and action of the non-active One.

The wholly spiritual Ones keep their eyes fixed constantly on their God while carrying the cares of the world. They keep their eyes constantly fixed on their God while living in and taking part in the world's activities.

Reality seeing Itself is spiritual vision. Reality must be seen as Reality sees Itself.

God demands that you live both individual and universal being.

It is not enough to pray even with great sincerity that God's will be done on earth. More is needed. You need to surrender your will to God. The only acceptable prayer is the rebirth of God's will in you. Being willing to do God's will is but the first step. You must do His will. You must live His will. You must be God-in-action. You must let God's will be done in you—as in heaven, so on earth.

Only the One can give you Oneness with Itself. Only the One can sustain your oneness.

All action is in the One. Let this One have your complete devotion. Let this One be your deepest love. Let this One be you as love actively expressed.

When you attain your oneness with the One, you will know the present reality of that which you previously believed to be the past, the present or the future. You will be the All. You will exist as you, your Self. Then you will not need to be known by others.

Eventually you must surrender all activity for the serenity of the One. You must become the non-doing Self responding to the ever-being One.

The One supplies all your needs. But your needs are not what you presently believe them to be.

Genuine peace will be found in the One—and only in the One.

The One lives in the soul of every creature.

Selfless love actively shared is ultimate Truth and the only source of genuine joy.

Genuine love is never received from people nor can it be given to people. Genuine love is not even expressed through the giving of things. Genuine love is received from God and must be given back to Him.

Love shared is the only love which is kept.

Every religious seeker should frequently ask himself: "Do I seek God so that I may serve Him or do I seek Him for his gifts?"

God is the power which makes the crooked places straight and the straight places crooked.

God is the great power in which all actions both material and spiritual find their source.

God can only be known as the human mind gives up its pretense of knowing.

Man reasons; God knows.

Love is God being Himself through us.

God is present in us only as love.

God being Himself is love.

Hatred is death, Love is life. Hatred is death to all that is of genuine value in life. Love is life to all that is of genuine value in life.

The One is. You as divine action and the you-in-action is your divine Self.

Christ Jesus declared that he was in the Father. Meditation is dwelling in your Father. Meditation is dwelling in the Source of your being and with all other living entities.

The human mind can play no part in genuine meditation. Like the wind, it is restless and undisciplined. But there is the wind of God which is ever moving in you. It is ever moving in you to bring you to your unity with your Father.

Lose yourself to find your Self. Lose yourself in order that your divine Self may be reborn.

When meditating you will find it helpful to let go of all thinking, all reasoning, all concepts, all images. Do not focus on an outside anything.

Be a listener. There is no separation between you and your Source. Your Source is ever talking to you. Just listen.

Church is really never a building. It is the home of divine Spirit. It is where the communion of saints takes place.

God is That which cannot be defined and cannot be understood through any definition of Him.

When there is warfare in families or among nations, one is unable to talk, understand or feel another's cares.

Never be so unkind to yourself that you ask to be delivered out of any problem until you have—with God's help—grappled with the problem and gained the lesson which the problem has for you.

Accepting another into our awareness leaves us free to influence another—either for good or evil—depending upon the goodness or evil of our view. Also, accepting another into our awareness has its effect for good or evil upon ourselves. Therefore, it behooves us to accept another into our awareness only so that we may bless, comfort and heal.

A guru must not be permitted to replace the inner guru. A church must not be permitted to replace the inner church. An organization must not be permitted to replace inner freedom. The external and material must not be permitted to replace the inner and spiritual.

Christ Jesus said: "Love your neighbor." He did not say "love your friend." You are to love those for whom you have no friendly feelings. You are to love your neighbor; and everyone, everywhere is to be your neighbor.

Lord, give me an individual who loves and I will speak to him of his indestructible relationship to the One.

The fire goes out when no new wood is added. The flame of divine inspiration goes out when no new daily inspiration is accepted.

The problems of the world are not your problems. All problems are God's problems. Only by accepting them and going through them can you be aware of the divine Source—the source of all, including problems.

You must stop thinking of the many. Only then can you be aware of the One—the unthinking, the unreasoning, the innumerable One.

Death is but the continuation of Life within.

Religion must not be used to avoid the facing up to the glory of death. Genuine religion is the good news which proclaims the eternality of the Life which includes in Itself that experience which we call death.

Reason causes you to labor for knowledge. Reason causes you to be bound and limited by systems and formulas. Your lifework is to free yourself from reason's knowledge, systems and formulas. Your lifework is to see the One as your limitless awareness.

Let yourself die before the death experience overtakes you and you will live forever.

You are to see all existence as beyond what the knowledge of the human mind can report to you and beyond what the physical senses can report to you.

You are destined to be wrapped in the garment of non-being.

The Holy Man is one who is a stranger to the world while still living in the world.

Daily you are dying and being reborn. Daily you are being renewed. Daily the One is showing you the majesty of who you are and what you are.

God should not be approached sentimentally. He is absolute Reality, the One and the All. He must be approached as the One, the All and as eternal Reality.

As you grow spiritually, meditation will be both easier and harder for you. But whether meditation is easier or harder is not what is important. The important thing is that you are being still enough to receive clearer views of who you are and where you are.

The one Spirit is in all things. All things are in the one Spirit.

You must learn to be complete joy. You must learn the joy of sameness and the joy of difference.

Prayer is a privilege not an obligation.

The greatest accomplishments in life are to be still enough so that you may hear God speak—and to act upon what you hear Him saying to you.

You are free but not independent. You are free to do God's will in His way, but not to do it in an independent manner.

You appear to destroy your individuality—not only by hatred—but also by indifference.

More than your mind, God desires your heart.

You should seek to discover "how" God is rather than "what" God is.

You ignorantly think that you have reached your divine destiny when you talk about the Self. But the very act of talking about the Self may separate you from your divine Self. You advance into the land of the unknown Self by living—not by speech. You must enter "the land ye know not of" (See Hebrews 11:8.) before you will be aware of your divine Self. Are you willing to enter this land?

There is but one world which you may view through a glass darkly or which you may view with the clarity of spiritual Awareness.

The One is all-pervading and self-existing.

Being aware of your divine Self includes being aware of universal oneness.

The One is both time which destroys and eternity which preserves.

The great Guru is God. Let Him teach you.

Let God renew and inspire you each time you read the Scriptures.

It is our own willfulness and not God which leads us into temptation. The prayer "Lead us not into temptation" should be used as: "Let us not be led into temptation." Don't let our willfulness tempt us to believe in more than the One.

Don't ask why another's actions bother you. Rather ask: "what is there in me that is bothered by another's actions?"

All individual life is part of the Whole. Therefore, to destroy any manifestation of life, however small, is to destroy the whole so far as you are concerned.

The soul which the One has given you is forever perfect and pure. Your life-work is to discover this soul.

Genuine faith has a holier basis than mere belief in a distorted view of external truth.

Everything you say and everything you do proceeds from the One.

Hate not those who hate you. If the one hating you is greater than you, your hatred will but increase his violence against you. If he is weaker than you, your hatred is unnecessary. Hence, do not hate. Always love.

The God-within will some day be recognized as the ever-healing Doctor.

He who gathers only for himself gathers for himself wrath against the day of wrath. This is true even though he may gather what he believes to be good and necessary things.

Be like a tree which gives shade even to those who cut off its boughs.

To spiritually meditate is to accept the light of the Fire which both purifies and enlightens.

Your beginning is your end and in your end is your beginning.

Divine Love sends you into the world, but does not give you to the world.

You have been given a body with which to serve others. You have been given a heart by which you may love others. But you have already been given spiritual awareness so that you may both serve and love.

The world is healthy; the disease is man.

Your spiritual identity is expressed as motion and motionlessness. It is far away and ever "at hand."

God in you and you in God are the genuine embodiment of spiritual perfection.

Birth and death. Unfortunately you think of them to be different.

The most dangerous thing you will ever do will be to share the Truth. But more dangerous than not sharing is the refusal to share the Truth. To genuinely share the Truth requires that one be the Truth himself.

God can never be found in a denial—not even a denial of evil. He can only be gained by living Him. The only valid denial is the denial of all denials.

Strictly speaking, God cannot give you your divine Self. What He gives you is the willingness to seek for it.

God within you welcomes the God coming to you. All there is is the one God recognizing the one God.

For spiritual development, better be two hours early than two minutes late.

Everything is God and God is everything; else God would not be the All.

Being a Mary to a Jesus is the message of Christmas.

W. NORMAN COOPER, an inspired Teacher, worldwide lecturer and author of numerous books, was born in Canada and spent his childhood in that country and in the United States. At an early age, he showed signs of remarkable spiritual gifts and he innately knew that he had a unique spiritual work to do.

As a young child, he became aware of his oneness with his God, and he wished to share this awareness with others. When he was a boy of ten, he began asking for a definition of God. When he saw, through his spiritual awareness, that God was beyond any explanation, he realized that God must be lived. If he could not tell others about God, he could show God's existence by his life of selfless service.

Through his great love and desire to serve others, Truth Center, a Universal Fellowship, was established in 1970 and his many messages given at the Center have been published in AGAPE, a periodical which is printed in many languages and distributed throughout the world. Under his guidance, the Fellowship is engaged in furthering a message of hope and encouragement for those who are searching for a new way of life.